THE
+BIG+
COUNT
DOWN
× + = −

SEVEN QUINTILLION, FIVE HUNDRED QUADRILLION GRAINS OF SAND ON PLANET EARTH

PAUL ROCKETT

W
FRANKLIN WATTS
LONDON•SYDNEY

First published in 2014 by Franklin Watts

Franklin Watts
338 Euston Road
London NW1 3BH

Franklin Watts Australia
Level 17/207 Kent Street
Sydney, NSW 2000

Editor: Rachel Cooke
Design and illustration: Mark Ruffle
www.rufflebrothers.com

Dewey number: 551
HB ISBN: 978 1 4451 2676 0
Library ebook: 978 1 4451 2682 1

Printed in China

Franklin Watts is a division of Hachette
Children's Books, an Hachette UK company.
www.hachette.co.uk

*Every attempt has been made to clear copyright.
Should there be any inadvertent omission please
apply to the publisher for rectification.*

Picture credits: AZ68/istockphoto: 21cr; beboy/
Shutterstock: front cover b; Wilyam Bradberry/
Shutterstock: front cover c; Mike Brake/Shutterstock:
10b; Ashley Cooper/Alamy: 5b; Jacques Descloitres,
MODIS Land Raid Response Teamat NASA/GSFC:
16c; Fisherrs/Shutterstock: front cover t; Oleg
Karpov/Shutterstock: 26br; lemga/istockphoto: 16t;
Lightspring/Shutterstock: 26bl; R. Lusak/Shutterstock:
19tr; Marafona/Shutterstock: 26tc; NASA: 4tl; Ocean
Image Photography/Shutterstock: 17b; Prometheus72/
Shutterstock: 23tr; Matt Ragen/Shutterstock: 26cl;
Slim Sepp/Shutterstock: 26cr; Graeme Shannon/
Shutterstock: 25tr; Nigel Spiers/Shutterstock: 23tl;
Michael Spooneybarger/Reuters/Corbis: 16b; Anibal
Trejo/Shutterstock: 11br; Vacclav/Shutterstock: 20b.

*Throughout the book you are given data relating
to various pieces of information covering the topic.
The numbers will most likely be an estimation based
on research made over a period of time and in a
particular area. Some other research may reach
a different set of data, and all these figures may
change with time as new research and information is
gathered. The numbers provided within this book are
believed to be correct at the time of printing and have
been sourced from the following sites:*
4thsummit.com; aquariumfishspecies.info; bbc.
co.uk; bgs.ac.uk; ces.fau.edu; dosomething.
org; earthobservatory.nasa.gov; earthquake.
usgs.gov; ecotricity.co.uk; edinburghgeolsoc.org;
en.worldstat.info; environment.nationalgeographic.
co.uk; factsanddetails.com; geology inmotion.
com; googology.wikia.com; graphs.net;
guinessworldrecords.com; kidsgeo.com; livescience.
com; marianatrench.com; mtkilimanjarologue.
com; nature.com; news.bbc.co.uk; nytimes.com;
oceanservice.noaa.gov; platetectonics.com; public.
asu.edu; pubs.usgs.gov; sciencedaily.com; sciencekids.
co.nz; science.nationalgeographic.co.uk; theguardian.
com; thesummitregister.com; svs.gasfc.nasa.gov;
ultimatekilimanjaro.com; un.org; universe-review.
ca; universetoday.com; usgs.gov; utahscience.
oremjr.alpine.k12.ut.us; volcanodiscovery.com;
weatherwizkids.com; worldwaterfalldatabase.com;
worldwildlife.org.

THE BIG COUNTDOWN
SEVEN QUINTILLION, FIVE HUNDRED QUADRILLION
GRAINS OF SAND ON PLANET EARTH

CONTENTS

NEPTUNE

Earth is the planet we live on.
Most geologists believe that the Earth is around **4,540,000,000 years old** and that it came into being from molten rocks flying through space and crashing into each other.

URANUS

CORES MIXING TOGETHER

SATURN

JUPITER

MARS

EARTH IS THE THIRD PLANET FROM THE SUN

Earth is **150,000,000 km** from the Sun. If it was any closer, the atmosphere could become too hot for life; any further away and the Earth might get too cold for life.

The Earth is constantly evolving. Over time it has established complex systems made up of water, land, air and life that all interact with each other and keep us alive. No other planet in the Solar System is known to have the ecosystems and life that are found on Earth.

EARTH

150,000,000 km from the Sun.

VENUS

MERCURY

The heat from the Sun is vital for life on Earth. The heat provides energy for plants to grow, and the plants become food for animals.

SUN

MOVING LAND

The Earth we recognise today, from images taken from space or maps, is very different to how it looked when Earth began. **225,000,000 years ago** the Earth was made up of one big ocean and a large mass of land. Over time, this land split and drifted to become what we see today.

225,000,000 years ago

200,000,000 years ago

135,000,000 years ago

65,000,000 years ago

North America
Asia
Africa
South America
Australia
Antarctica

Present day

WHAT IS A GEOLOGIST?

Geologists are scientists who specialise in studying the structure of the Earth and the forces that have changed it over time. This includes the study of rocks, earthquakes, volcanoes, soil and fossils. By studying Earth's materials they are able to date the age of the planet and investigate how it came into being.

PLANET EARTH CONTINUES TO CHANGE

Geologists study the planet to tell us more about its past, which helps to tell us about what may occur in the future. For example, by studying coastal rocks and soil, geologists have been able to calculate how sea levels have changes over Earth's history.

SEA LEVEL CHANGE THROUGH TIME

Cambrian 542,000,000 years ago
Ordovician 488,000,000 years ago
Silurian 444,000,000 years ago
Devonian 416,000,000 years ago
Carboniferous 359,000,000 years ago
Permian 299,000,000 years ago
Triassic 251,000,000 years ago
Jurassic 200,000,000 years ago
Cretaceous 145,000,000 years ago
Palaeogene 65,000,000 years ago
Neogene 23,000,000 years ago

Sea level change in metres: 400, 300, 200, 100, 0, -100

The changes in sea level occur due to an increase in the Earth's temperature, which causes ocean water to expand.

TUVALU ISLAND

The impact of natural disasters, such as hurricanes, and the effects of climate change, are causing sea levels to rise again and land mass to reduce. This has caused the island of Tuvalu, in the Pacific, to be only **2 m** above sea level. Some geologists expect Tuvalu to disappear under water within the next **20 years**.

THERE ARE ABOUT 200 TREDECILLION ATOMS IN EARTH'S ATMOSPHERE

Everything around you is made up of atoms.
The only thing smaller than an atom is the subatomic particles that make up an atom.

● ·· NEUTRON ··
● ·· PROTON ··
● ·· ELECTRON ··

The three major subatomic particles that make up an atom are neutrons, protons and electrons.

Some scientists think that there are about **200 tredecillion atoms** in the Earth's atmosphere. Written as a number, that looks like this:

200,000,000,000,000,000,000,000,000,000,000,000,000,000,000

WHAT IS THE ATMOSPHERE?

The Earth's atmosphere is the area of space that surrounds and protects the Earth. It contains the gases essential for life on Earth. It also absorbs harmful gases.

THERE ARE FIVE LAYERS TO THE EARTH'S ATMOSPHERE:

5. EXOSPHERE ····· 500–8,000 km

4. THERMOSPHERE ··· 80–500 km

3. MESOSPHERE ········ 50–80 km

2. STRATOSPHERE ······· 8–50 km
1. TROPOSPHERE ········· 0–8 km
at the North Pole

70 kg

The number of atoms thought to be in a human being weighing **70 kg** is **seven octillion**. Written as a number, that looks like this:

7,000,000,000,000,000,000,000,000,000

TROPOSPHERE
0 – 16 km at the Equator

EARTH

EQUATOR

GRAVITY
All objects have a force that pulls them towards each other. This is called gravity.

THE FIVE LAYERS OF THE EARTH'S ATMOSPHERE:

5. EXOSPHERE
Temperature: 2,200°C+
The exosphere has no clear limit, gradually fading into outer space. The air pressure and pull of the Earth's gravity here is so weak that atoms drift off into outer space.

4. THERMOSPHERE
Temperature: minus 80°C–2,200°C
The thermosphere is a large layer with a wide range in temperature. The temperature rises sharply towards its outer layer, as it absorbs a lot of the Sun's radiation.

3. MESOSPHERE
Temperature: 10 °C– minus 90°C
The coldest temperatures in the Earth's atmosphere are at the top of the mesosphere layer, where the Sun's radiation cools.

RADIATION
Radiation from the Sun is a mixture of electromagnetic waves and the sunlight that we see. Too much of these waves, such as ultraviolet rays, can be harmful to a balanced climate on Earth. The atmosphere is important in absorbing the harmful rays, acting as a protective barrier.

WEATHER
The troposphere is where clouds form and where rain falls. It is the only layer that contains enough water vapour to make clouds. If all the water came down in one go, it would cover the Earth's surface with **2.5 cm** of water.

40 tonnes of meteors crash into the mesosphere daily. They burn out in this layer before getting any closer to Earth.

2. STRATOSPHERE
Temperature: minus 55°C–10 °C
The stratosphere is very dry and contains little water vapour. Because of this, few clouds form here and so many aircraft fly in this layer.

1. TROPOSPHERE
Temperature: minus 55°C–15°C
The troposphere is made up of **21%** oxygen. Oxygen is the gas that we breathe in to keep ourselves alive.

GASES IN THE TROPOSPHERE:

78% nitrogen
21% oxygen

0.9% argon
0.03% carbon dioxide
0.07% other gases including neon, helium, hydrogen and ozone

The larger the object, the larger the gravitational pull towards it. The Earth has a strong gravitational force that helps keep the layers of the atmosphere in place, surrounding it.

The Earth has a surface area of five hundred and ten quintillion mm².
As numbers, this figure is written as: **510,072,000,000,000,000,000 mm².**
Converted into kilometres squared this figure loses 12 zeros: **510,072,000 km².**
The size of the area remains the same, but the unit of measurement is greater.

NOT QUITE ROUND

The Earth is not a perfect sphere. Its diameter and circumference vary depending on where you take the measurement. **The diameter** is a straight line that runs through the centre of a shape, from one side to the other.

Diameter

Circumference

The circumference is the distance around an object.

. . . .

There are two lines of measurement that are used for the Earth:

MAPPING THE EARTH

The shape of the Earth means that showing it on a flat surface, like a map, distorts it in some way. Because of this there are many different ways in which it can be shown:

Mercator Projection
This map has flattened the Earth into a grid of straight lines, making countries towards the North and South poles much larger than they are in real life.

Mollweide Projection
Here the Earth is presented as an ellipse to show the land masses in proportion to each other. However, this changes the angle and shape of the countries.

Goode's Homolosine Equal-area Projection
This map is laid out to take into account the curved shape of the Earth, breaking it up into related areas. This reproduces the size and shape of land masses as acurately as possible.

Dymaxion Map
This map can be folded together to form the three-dimensional shape of an icosahedron. It has minimal distortion to the size and shape of countries and does not present the Earth as having one 'right way up'.

The Equator
Diameter: **12,756 km**
Circumference: **40,075 km**

From the North Pole to the South Pole
Diameter: **12,713 km**
Circumference: **40,007 km**

Equator

North to South Pole

The difference between the two diameter measurements is a distance of **43 km**.

The difference between the two circumference measurements is a distance of **68 km**.

DIVIDING UP THE EARTH

The Earth is divided in different ways, indicating such things as time zones, climates and the boundaries of countries and continents.

LATITUDE AND LONGITUDE

The vertical lines on a map are known as lines of longitude. The horizontal lines on a map are known as lines of latitude. These lines help people navigate. The circles of latitude also act as a division of climate zones.

EARTH'S HEMISPHERES

The Earth is halved into the Northern Hemisphere and Southern Hemisphere. The line that marks this division is the Equator. There are different weather patterns in the Northern and Southern hemispheres because of the Earth's seasonal tilt towards and away from the Sun.

THE EARTH IS DIVIDED INTO FIVE MAIN CIRCLES OF LATITUDE:

1. Arctic Circle
2. Tropic of Cancer
3. Equator
4. Tropic of Capricorn
5. Antarctic Circle

TIME

The Sun rises and sets at different points in the day around the world. The Earth has been divided into time zones at **15 degree** distances from each other, ensuring that it is noon when the Sun is highest in the sky for each zone. There are **24 time zones**, one for each hour of the day. These are measured from the Prime Meridian and the International Date Line, which are lines that divide the Earth into an Eastern and a Western hemisphere.

TWO POLES

The Earth has two geographic poles, one at each end of its axis, where all the points of longitude meet: the North Pole and the South Pole.

N The North Pole is in the middle of the Arctic Ocean.

S The South Pole is in the Antarctic.

Prime Meridian

International Date Line

If you call at 12 midday from London, UK, to someone in New York, USA, the time there will be 7.00am.

It has been estimated that there are 7,500,000,000,000,000,000 grains of sand on Earth. This calculation has been made by working out an average size of a grain of sand and calculating how many of these grains can fit into a teaspoon. The amount of sand within this teaspoon has then been multiplied by the size of all the beaches and deserts in the world.

WHAT IS SAND?

Sand is made up of tiny pieces of rock, minerals and fossils that have been eroded down in size by the weather and movements of the sea.

Pebbles
4–64 mm

Granules
2–4 mm

Coarse sand
0.5–2 mm

Medium sand
0.25–0.5 mm

Fine sand
0.06–0.25 mm

Clay
<0.004 mm

Sand grains range in size but are smaller than granules and larger than clay.

BEACHES

Not all beaches have sand along the shoreline. They can also be composed of gravel, pebbles or shells. Beach materials are often products of erosion, where waves have beaten against the coastline causing small rocks to come loose. Tides also carry sediment to the shore; this may include shells and seaweed.

Some volcanic islands, such as Hawaii, may have black beaches, with the shore covered in fragments of basalt and lava from a volcanic eruption.

PUNALUU BEACH, HAWAII

EROSION

Coastlines are always changing. The waves erode the rocks on the cliffs, creating sea caves, arches and stacks.

Cave

Arch

Arch collapses

Stack

LONGEST BEACHES IN THE WORLD

Praia do Cassino Beach, Brazil

Cox's Bazar, Bangladesh

Padre Island, Texas

Ninety Mile Beach, Australia

Ninety Mile Beach, New Zealand*

| 0 | 20 | 40 | 60 | 80 | 100 | 120 | 140 | 160 | 180 | 200 | 220 | 240 | 260 |

Beach length in km

*Although named Ninety Mile Beach, this beach in New Zealand is actually around **88 miles long**.

The tallest sandcastle in the world was built in May 2011 in Connecticut, USA. It measured **11.53 m**. That's almost as tall as **three double-decker buses**.

DESERT SANDS

Deserts make up around **9.5%** of the world's surface. Only **20%** of the deserts in the world are covered by sand. The rest are covered with rocks, pebbles and different types of soil.

The Sahara Desert is the largest sand-filled desert on Earth.

DESERTS ········▶

100% OF EARTHS SURFACE

70.8% WATER ···········

·········· 29.2% LAND ·········

Weather is all around us. Whatever is happening in the air, such as the level of visibility, the heat, rain or wind, it is a weather condition.

THE SUN

The Sun's energy heats up some parts of the Earth more than others. This unequal heating creates variations in temperature, air pressure, winds and ocean currents. These elements move temperatures around the Earth, which in turn impact upon levels of moisture in the atmosphere, rain and cloud formations.

The Sun's radiation heats up the air.

Hot air has a low density and rises.

The hot air carries water vapour with it, which expands, cools and condenses to form clouds.

Heavy, low, cool air blows in to take the place of hot air, causing wind.

OCEAN CURRENTS

There are ocean currents around the Earth, which act like vast rivers moving water around. They are caused by intensities of temperature, wind and tide. These currents transport hot and cold water, which affects local temperatures. They are also incredibly important for marine ecosystems, delivering nutrients to marine life across the ocean.

The largest current is the Great Ocean Conveyor Belt. This carries warmer, less salty water from the Equator towards the poles, and colder, saltier water from the poles back towards the Equator. This current circulates the globe in a **1,000 year cycle**.

AIR PRESSURE

Air pressure is the weight of air pressing in all around us. The difference in pressure from one area to another causes air to move about, with this air being what we recognise as wind.

Great Ocean Conveyor Belt

CLOUDS

Clouds form within the troposphere and occur when the air cannot hold any more water vapour. Clouds come in different shapes depending on the temperature, height and movement of air around them.

Cirrus: dry, sunny weather

Cirrocumulus: warm weather with rain and thunder ahead

Cumulonimbus: heavy rain, thunderstorms, hail, tornadoes

Altocumulus: cool weather with thunderstorms ahead

Altostratus: storms ahead

Stratus: fog, drizzle or snow

Stratocumulus: dry, settled weather to light rain and snow

Cumulus: fair weather

Cloud height in km

16 — 15 — 6 — 5 — 4 — 3 — 2 — 1 — 0

EXTREME WEATHER

We largely experience stable weather conditions with periods of sunshine, rain or snow, that is factored into how we live our daily lives. However, weather can be unpredictable and cause a lot of damage to buildings and the environment.

HURRICANES

A hurricane is a destructive storm that gathers over a warm part of the ocean.

Water vapour rises to condense into a large cloud. Cool air currents spin the cloud around like a wheel. The speed of these currents can rise to over **250 km/h** and can carry the hurricane to the coast and on to land.

TORNADOES

Tornadoes are the fastest winds on Earth, capable of carrying large objects over land, spinning at speeds of up to **550 km/h**.

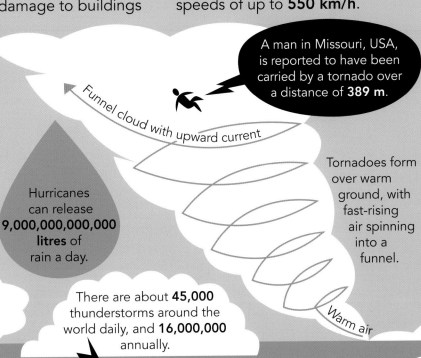

A man in Missouri, USA, is reported to have been carried by a tornado over a distance of **389 m**.

Funnel cloud with upward current

Tornadoes form over warm ground, with fast-rising air spinning into a funnel.

Warm air

Cool dense air

Eye

Warm moist air

Hurricanes can release **9,000,000,000,000 litres** of rain a day.

There are about **45,000** thunderstorms around the world daily, and **16,000,000** annually.

OVER SEVEN BILLION PEOPLE ON PLANET EARTH

There are over 7,000,000,000 people living on Earth. It's been estimated that by 2050 there will be more than **9,000,000,000 people** calling Earth their home.

THE HUMAN POPULATION HAS MORE THAN DOUBLED IN THE LAST 50 YEARS.

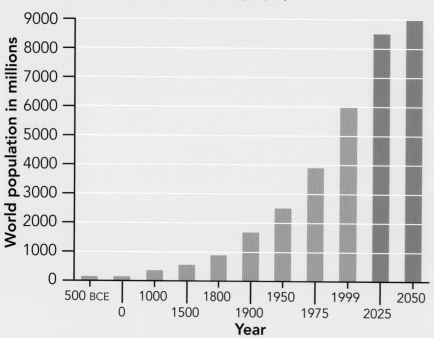

The reason for the rapid growth in human population is through improvements in medicine and developments in food production, ensuring healthier lifestyles. Because of this, many people are living longer.

APPROXIMATELY 4.45 BABIES ARE BORN EVERY SECOND.

This calculation comes from the figure of **267 babies** being born every minute. When a calculation provides a decimal number (.45), it is usual to round up or down. Here we would say four babies, or use an example where this can be avoided and there is no decimal, such as: **89 babies** born every **20 seconds**.

BIRTH

In America, in the 1900s, the average life expectancy of a man was **46 years**, and **48 years** for a woman. By 2011 an American male could expect to live for a further **30 years**, and a woman a further **43 years**.

1900 average American male

1900 average American female

1950 average American male

1950 average American female

2011 average American male

2011 average American female

HUMAN LIFESPAN IN YEARS

90 years

THERE ARE 196 COUNTRIES IN THE WORLD SPREAD OVER SEVEN CONTINENTS.

Largest
continent: Asia
44,537,920 km²

Smallest
continent:
Australasia
8,564,400 km²

RUSSIA

Largest country:
Russia: 148,940,00 km²
It crosses Asia and Europe.

Smallest country:
Vatican City: 0.44 km²

You could fit approximately
38,781,175 countries the
size of Vatican City
into Russia.

1. ASIA
Area: 44,537,920 km²
Population: 4,175,332,754
Male: 2,131,947,122
Female: 2,043,385,632

2. AFRICA
Area: 30,311,690 km²
Population: 1,037,694,509
Male: 518,636,010
Female: 519,058,499

3. NORTH AMERICA
Area: 22,656,190 km²
Population: 544,774,178
Male: 268,298,759
Female: 276,475,419

4. SOUTH AMERICA:
Area: 17,866,130 km²
Population: 400,103,516
Male: 197,745,352
Female: 202,358,164

5. EUROPE
Area: 10,205,720 km²
Population: 734,228,971
Male: 354,542,772
Female: 380,686,199

6. AUSTRALASIA
Area: 8,564,400 km²
Population: 35,162,670
Male: 17,699,546
Female: 17,463,124

7. ANTARCTICA
Area: 13,340,000 km²
Population: there are no
permanent human residents
here, but around 4,000
scientists stay here over the
course of a year.

11,030 METRES DOWN TO THE DEEPEST PART OF THE OCEAN

The surface of the Earth is 70.8% water, with the rest being land.

68.3% SALTWATER

The majority of the water on Earth is found in the oceans. The water here is saltwater which can also be found in inland seas and some lakes.

We cannot drink saltwater because of the high level of salt it contains. In every **1 l** of seawater there is approximately **35 g** of salt, which is around **2 heaped tablespoons**.

2.5% FRESHWATER

The majority of freshwater is locked into the ice caps and glaciers but can also be found in lakes, rivers and underground. This is the water that we can drink.

41%

Not all marine life lives in saltwater. Around **41%** of known species of fish are found only in freshwater.

68.3% SALTWATER
2.5% FRESHWATER

WATER: 29.2%
LAND: 70.8%

The whale shark is the largest saltwater fish and can grow up to **12 m in length**. They have a mouth that can be up to **1.5 m wide**. That's almost as long as the height of an average man. Despite their size, however, they only feed on tiny fish, small plants and plankton.

1.76 m   1.5 m

LAKE BAIKAL FROM ABOVE

The oldest lake in the world, Lake Baikal in Russia, is over **25,000,000 years old** and contains **one-fifth** of the Earth's freshwater.

The largest freshwater fish is the beluga sturgeon. It lives in both freshwater and saltwater. It can measure up to **5 m** in length and weigh up to **1,133 kg**. They can live up to **11 years of age**.

THERE ARE FIVE OCEANS ON PLANET EARTH.

Arctic Ocean 14,056,000 km²

Pacific Ocean 155,557,000 km²

Atlantic Ocean 76,762,000 km²

Indian Ocean 68,556,000 km²

Mariana Trench

Southern Ocean 20,327,000 km²

Depth/Height in km

Sea level

Mariana Trench

Mount Everest

The deepest part of the ocean is the Mariana Trench. It is also the deepest location on Earth, at just over **11 km deep**. If the tallest point on Earth, Mount Everest, were set in this trench, then only **2.1 km** would poke above sea level.

THE ANGLER FISH
One of the creatures that lives in the deepest part of the Mariana Trench is the angler fish. Its mouths is so big that it can swallow food up to twice its size.

FIVE LARGEST SEAS

Barents Sea, Arctic Ocean

Mediterranean Sea, Atlantic Ocean

South China Sea, Pacific Ocean

Arabian Sea, Indian Ocean

Weddell Sea, Southern Ocean

SEAS
We describe the body of water in the ocean as 'seawater' but we also use the term 'sea' for smaller areas of water in the ocean and also some areas of water inland.

| 0 | 1,000,000 | 2,000,000 | 3,000,000 | 4,000,000 | 5,000,000 | 6,000,000 | 7,000,000 | 8,000,000 |

Size in km²

EARLIEST ANIMAL LIFE FORMS
Sea sponges are among the first forms of animal life on Earth. Scientists have discovered fossilised evidence to suggest that they have been around for over **760,000,000,000 years**.

THE LONGEST RIVER MEASURES 6,650 KM

The longest river in the world is the River Nile in Africa, measuring 6,650 km.

LONGEST RIVERS

Nile, Africa

Amazon, South America

Yangtze, Asia

Mississippi, North America

0   1,000   2,000   3,000   4,000   5,000   6,000   7,000

River length in km

JOURNEY OF A RIVER

Rivers can form and travel over great distances before joining up with the sea.

Rain collects and soaks into the ground through soil and rocks, and can rise up and gather together to form a spring in hills and mountains.

Many streams join together to make a river. Streams and rivers that flow into a river are called tributaries.

As the river flows through flatter land it becomes wider and slow-moving. The river loops over the land. These loops are called meanders.

A spring trickles down to become a stream.

A meander may get separated from the main river channel to form an oxbow lake.

Where the river meets the sea is the river mouth. It may be a wide channel called an estuary or a group of sandy islands called a delta.

WATERFALLS

Waterfalls wear away the rocks they flow over. As the rocks wear away, the waterfall moves position.

10,000 years ago, Niagara Falls was **11 km** further downstream, but over time the water has eroded the rock, and continues to do so.

HARD ROCK

PLUNGE POOL

Depletion of rock from Niagara over time.

1886
1842
1819
1764
1678

WATER CYCLE

The water cycle is the process that water goes through, circulating from the land to the sky and back again. Rivers, seas and oceans are key to this cycle.

Water evaporates, rising and condensing to form clouds.

The Sun heats up the sea.

Clouds cool, releasing water as rain, snow, sleet or hail.

Overground river

Underground flow

The water that collects at the top of mountainous areas, in springs or as snow, runs downhill, forming rivers that flow into the sea.

Angel Falls, Venezuela
Tugela, South Africa

Utigord, Norway

HIGHEST WATERFALL

The world's highest waterfall is Angel Falls in Venezuela, with a height of **979 m**.

1,000
900
800
700
600
500
400
300
200
100
0

Waterfall height in metres

Saint Benedict
A Catholic Voluntary Academy
Duffield Road, Darley Abbey
Derby
DE22 1JD

A volcano is a mountain or a hill that has an opening through which hot molten rock and gas is pushed through from below the surface of the Earth.

ACTIVE

A volcano is defined as active if it has erupted within the last **10,000 years**. **1,510 volcanoes** have erupted in the last **10,000 years**.

DORMANT

A volcano is described as dormant if it has not erupted within the last **10,000 years** but is expected to erupt again.

EXTINCT

A volcano is described as extinct if it is expected never to erupt again.

THERE ARE THREE TYPES OF VOLCANO:

Composite volcano

Cinder cone volcano

Shield volcano

AROUND THE WORLD

75% of the world's active volcanoes are in the Ring of Fire around the Pacific Ocean.

Indonesia has **76** active volcanoes.

There are more than **80** volcanoes under the ocean.

MOUNT VESUVIUS, 79 BCE

One of the most famous volcanic eruptions occurred in 79 BCE. Mount Vesuvius, near Naples in Italy, erupted causing huge clouds of ash to rise into the air and bury the city of Pompeii.

In 1748, Pompeii was excavated revealing the city to be mostly intact. The volcanic ash that had covered the city created hollow mounds from which plaster casts were made. These casts revealed the shapes of people who had died there.

Over **1,150 bodies** have been discovered at the site of Pompeii.

SMOKE AND ASH

CRATER

LAVA

MAIN VENT

SIDE VENT

ERUPTIONS

Eruptions from volcanoes can involve gases or lava. Lava begins as magma that is found below the Earth's surface. Through high pressure and hot temperatures, magma pools into magma chambers. A large accumulation forces pressure upwards, pushing gases and magma upwards, creating volcanic eruptions.

MOST ACTIVE

STROMBOLI

Stromboli, a small island north of Sicily, has one of the world's most active volcanoes. It releases small explosions every **20–30 minutes**.

MAGMA CHAMBER

EARTH'S CRUST

THERE ARE 16 TECTONIC PLATES

The Earth's crust is made up of flat pieces of rock, called tectonic plates.
These plates move around slowly, but when they meet up at fault lines they create waves of energy that come up to the Earth's surface, causing an earthquake.

THERE ARE 16 MAJOR PLATES ON THE SURFACE OF THE EARTH.

Juan de Fuca Plate
North American Plate
Caribbean Plate
Eurasian Plate
Arabian Plate
Indian Plate
Philippine Plate
Pacific Plate
Cocos Plate
Pacific Plate
Nazca Plate
South American Plate
African Plate
Indo-Australian Plate
Antarctica Plate
Scotia Plate

BOUNDARIES

The movements of the tectonic plates against each other are categorised as three different boundaries:

Divergent boundary: where two plates pull apart from each other.

Convergent boundary: where two plates crash into each other.

Transform boundary: where two plates rub against each other.

Fault line
Epicentre
Focus
Seismic waves

An earthquake starts at its focus, with seismic waves (also known as shock waves) moving from the focus in all directions. Where the seismic waves reach the surface is called the epicentre – this is where the greatest shaking occurs.

Around **500,000 earthquakes** happen every year, but hardly any of them are felt by people.

MEASURING EARTHQUAKES

The Richter Scale was developed by Charles Richter in 1935 to measure the size of earthquakes. The higher the number the more destructive the earthquake.

RICHTER SCALE:

Level 9
GREAT
Can cause major destruction over huge areas

Level 8
MAJOR
Serious damage over large areas

Level 7
STRONG
Affects areas up to 100 km across

Level 6
MODERATE
Affects small regions, causing slight damage

Level 5
LIGHT
Damage only to weak buildings near the epicentre

Level 4
MINOR
Minor damage near the epicentre

Level 3
MICRO
Not generally felt

TSUNAMIS

The word tsunami is Japanese and means 'big wave in the port'. These largely occur due to earthquakes, when the epicentre is near to the seabed and the quake measures **7 or more** on the Richter Scale. The energy released pushes a mass of seawater up and down.

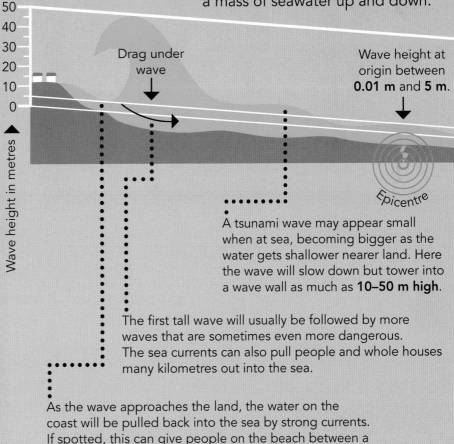

Drag under wave

Wave height at origin between **0.01 m** and **5 m**.

Wave height in metres

Epicentre

A tsunami wave may appear small when at sea, becoming bigger as the water gets shallower nearer land. Here the wave will slow down but tower into a wave wall as much as **10–50 m high**.

The first tall wave will usually be followed by more waves that are sometimes even more dangerous. The sea currents can also pull people and whole houses many kilometres out into the sea.

As the wave approaches the land, the water on the coast will be pulled back into the sea by strong currents. If spotted, this can give people on the beach between a few minutes to half an hour to escape to higher ground.

A **50 m wave** would be roughly the equivalent height to **27.5 men**.

Where tectonic plates have crashed into each other, mountain ranges have formed. The crust at the edge of the plates crumple and fold, pushing up the mountains.

YOUNG AND TALL

The youngest mountains on Earth are also the highest mountains. They have jagged peaks which, unlike the older mountains, have yet to be worn down by the weather.

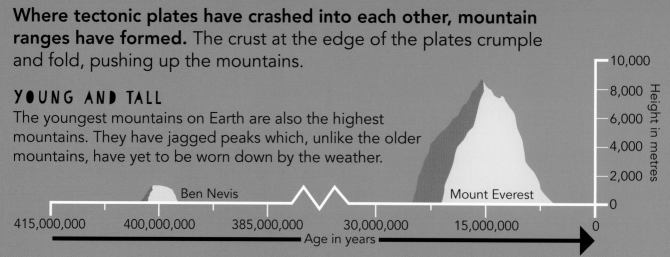

Mount Everest, at **8,848 m**, is a young mountain formed **15,000,000 years ago**, compared with Ben Nevis in Scotland, at **1,344 m**, which was formed over **400,000,000 years ago**.

TALLEST MOUNTAINS

LHOTSE
(border of Nepal and Tibet)
8,516 m

MAKALU
(border of Nepal and Tibet)
8,485 m

MAUNA KEA
(Hawaii)
10,203 m
(4,205 m above sea level)

KANGCHENJUNGA
(border of Nepal and India)
8,586 m

K2
(border of Pakistan and China)
8,611 m

MOUNT EVEREST
(border of Nepal and Tibet)
8,848 m

If we were to measure mountains from the seabed up, Mauna Kea would be the highest mountain in the world.

SMALLEST MOUNTAIN
148 m

There is no universally agreed height as to what makes a mountain. However, the world's smallest registered mountain is Mount Wycheproof in Australia, which reaches **148 m** in height. The Eiffel Tower in Paris is over twice as high.

MOUNT KILIMANJARO

Mount Kilimanjaro in Tanzania is the highest mountain in Africa. It is **5,895 m high**.

SUCCESS FAILURE

Approximately **25,000 people** attempt to climb to the top every year. Around two-thirds are successful.

ICE CAP

Mount Kilimanjaro has an ice cap at its top that was formed over **11,000 years ago**. An increase in temperature in the region has meant that the ice cap is melting.

80% OF THE ICE HAS DISAPPEARED

In the last century **80%** of the ice has disappeared, with some scientists predicting that the rest will disappear within **20 years**.

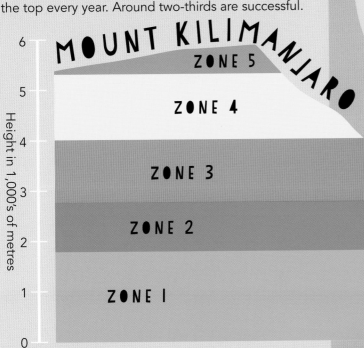

MOUNT KILIMANJARO

Height in 1,000's of metres

ZONE 5
ZONE 4
ZONE 3
ZONE 2
ZONE 1

Mount Kilimanjaro is known as the 'mountain of contrasts' as it contains a wide variety of ecosystems divided into **five zones**, that you pass on your way to the summit.

ZONE 1: FARMLAND 0–1,800 m

Area made up of farmland and small villages, where coffee and banana plantations are cultivated. Includes many streams and rivers.

ZONE 2: RAINFOREST 1,800 m–2,800 m

An area of lush, dense vegetation from heavy rainfall, this zone is home to olive baboons, giraffes, black rhinoceros, elephants and leopards.

ZONE 3: HEATH 2,800 m–4,000 m

The main vegetation in this area is heathers and mosses with the land having boggy patches of soil. Some elephants and leopards can be found roaming in the area, which also provides shelter for many birds, such as bearded vultures and crowned eagles.

ZONE 4: ALPINE DESERT 4,000 m–5,029 m

This region has little water and only a few grasses and small flowers are able to flourish in small areas.

ZONE 5: ARCTIC 5,029 m–5,895 m

Although this area experiences heavy winds, oxygen levels are nearly half that of sea level with lichen the only plant life that is able to grow here.

THREE TYPES OF ROCK

There are three types of rock: metamorphic, igneous and sedimentary. These rocks transform over long periods of time and through the processes of melting, cooling, erosion, pressure and compacting.

THE ROCK CYCLE

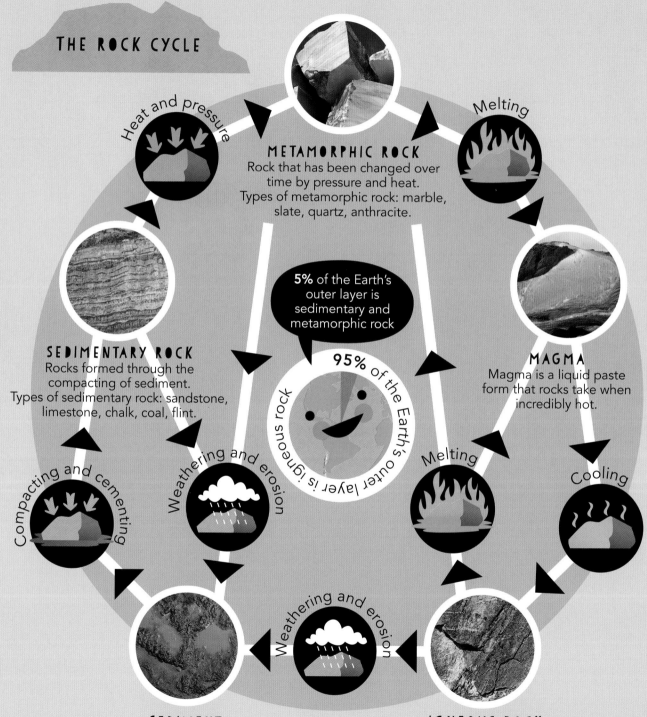

Heat and pressure

Melting

METAMORPHIC ROCK
Rock that has been changed over time by pressure and heat.
Types of metamorphic rock: marble, slate, quartz, anthracite.

5% of the Earth's outer layer is sedimentary and metamorphic rock

95% of the Earth's outer layer is igneous rock

SEDIMENTARY ROCK
Rocks formed through the compacting of sediment.
Types of sedimentary rock: sandstone, limestone, chalk, coal, flint.

MAGMA
Magma is a liquid paste form that rocks take when incredibly hot.

Compacting and cementing

Weathering and erosion

Melting

Cooling

Weathering and erosion

SEDIMENT
Sediment is material that has been broken down into tiny pieces, often to a state of liquid.

IGNEOUS ROCK
Rock created by the cooling of molten magma.
Types of igneous rock: basalt, granite, pumice, obsidian.

MINERALS

Rocks are made from two or more minerals. There are about **3,000 known minerals** on Earth. Many minerals form beautiful crystals and some are valued as gemstones that are used in jewellery.

Diamonds are the world's most popular gemstone. Around **26,000 kg** of diamonds are mined around the world every year.

COAL AND FOSSIL FUELS

Coal is a sedimentary rock. We burn coal as fuel to generate electricity. Coal was formed millions of year ago underground and because of this, and because of its use, it is known as a fossil fuel. Oil and natural gas are also fossil fuels that have been formed in a similar way.

Fossil fuels are not an infinite resource. Some scientists predict that they will be all used up by the end of this century.

All oil gone by 2052

All gas gone by 2060

All gone by 2088

2000   2020   2040   2060   2080   2010

Years

RENEWABLE ENERGY

With fossil fuels reaching their limit, we need to increase our use of natural renewable energy sources, such as solar power, wind power and hydropower.

FORMATION OF FOSSIL FUELS

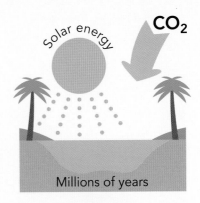

Solar energy CO_2

Millions of years

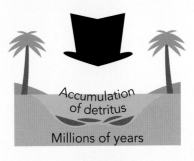

Accumulation of detritus

Millions of years

Dead animals and plants buried under sediment

Heat and pressure over millions of years

Natural gas   Oil   Coal

CO_2

About 100 years

ONE CORE AT THE CENTRE OF THE EARTH

The Earth is made up of four
main layers: crust, mantle,
outer core, and inner core.

CRUST

MANTLE

OUTER CORE

INNER CORE

TEMPERATURE OF
EARTH'S LAYERS:

Inner core
5,000–7,000 ^{o}C

Outer core
4,000–5,000 ^{o}C

Mantle
2,200–3,700 ^{o}C

Crust 55 ^{o}C

CRUST 7–100 km thick

The crust is the outer layer of the Earth upon which we live. The crust, measured from the ocean, is known as the oceanic crust and is only about **7 km deep**. Measured from the land, the continental crust, it can range in depth from **25 to 100 km**.

MANTLE 2,900 km thick

The mantle is made up of thick slow-moving lava. The flowing liquid in the mantle layer creates electric currents that generate a magnetic field around the Earth. The Earth has two magnetic poles that are in different positions to the geographic poles.

OUTER CORE 2,200 km thick

The outer core is made up of iron and nickel.

INNER CORE
1,250 km thick
This is the hottest part of the Earth, as hot as the surface of the Sun.

The magnetic north pole moves around, moving northward at about **64 km per year**. The magnetic poles attract a magnetic needle in a compass. This helps you to locate positions and travel around the Earth.

The Earth's inner core is **two thirds** the size of the Moon.

INNER CORE

The mantle comprises approximately 85% of the Earth's mass.

FURTHER INFORMATION

BOOKS

Navigators: Planet Earth by Barbara Taylor, (Kingfisher, 2012)
The Story of Planet Earth by Abigail Wheatley (Usbourne, 2013)
The World of Infographics: Planet Earth by Jon Richards and Ed Simkins (Wayland, 2013)
This Is My Planet by Jon Thornhill (Franklin Watts, 2012)

WEBSITES

Games, videos, photos and news on the inhabitants and geology of planet Earth:
kids.nationalgeographic.com/kids/
Information and links to videos and songs on the layers of the Earth, volcanoes and earthquakes:
www.kidsgeo.com/geology-for-kids/0037-the-earth-earth-inside-out.php
Character-led site that provides information and games explaining the role of geologists and their field of study:
www.onegeology.org/extra/kids/what_is.html

Note to parents and teachers:
Every effort has been made by the publisher to ensure that these websites contain no inappropriate or offensive material. However, because of the nature of the Internet, it is impossible to guarantee that the content of these sites will not be altered. We strongly advise that Internet access is supervised by a responsible adult.

LARGE NUMBERS

1,000,000,000,000,000,000,000,000,000,000,000 = ONE DECILLION
1,000,000,000,000,000,000,000,000,000,000 = ONE NONILLION
1,000,000,000,000,000,000,000,000,000 = ONE OCTILLION
1,000,000,000,000,000,000,000,000 = ONE SEPTILLION
1,000,000,000,000,000,000,000 = ONE SEXTILLION
1,000,000,000,000,000,000 = ONE QUINTILLION
1,000,000,000,000,000 = ONE QUADRILLION
1,000,000,000,000 = ONE TRILLION
1,000,000,000 = ONE BILLION
1,000,000 = ONE MILLION
1000 = ONE THOUSAND
100 = ONE HUNDRED
10 = TEN
1 = ONE

GLOSSARY

atmosphere	air in a particular place, such as the gases that surround the Earth
atom	smallest particle of a chemical element
average	usual amount, or an estimated or calculated means of division to find the middle number of a set
circumference	distance around an object, particularly the surrounding edge of a circle
climate	average weather conditions in a particular area
current	body of water or air continually moving in the same direction
crust	solid outer part of the Earth's surface
depletion	reduction in quantity of something
detritus	waste matter, generally produced by erosion
diameter	straight line passing from side to side through the centre of an object
earthquake	violent shaking of the ground caused by movements of the Earth's crust that can lead to the break up of the Earth's surface
ecosystem	community of organisms interacting within an environment
epicentre	point at which an earthquake reaches the Earth's surface
equator	an imaginary line drawn around the Earth separating the Northern and Southern hemispheres
erosion	wearing away of the Earth's surface by wind or water
fossil fuel	fuel made up of the remains of living things that have been compacted underground for thousands of years
gravity	a force that pulls objects together
hemisphere	half of a sphere, such as sections of the Earth divided by the Equator or line from the North to the South Pole
hurricane	storm with a strong and violent wind
igneous rock	rock formed by the solidification of molten magma
latitude	distances measured north and south of the Equator, often visualised in horizontal lines
life expectancy	the average amount of years which something is expected to live
longitude	vertical lines used to measure distances
magma	molten rock that lies under the Earth's crust
meander	winding bends of a river
metamorphic rock	rock that has been formed by extreme heat and pressure
minerals	solid, inorganic substance that are often found underground
molten	fused or liquified by heat
oxbow lake	lake formed from a bend in the river, where the river has cut across the narrow end of a loop in the bend
radiation	energy transmitted as waves
sediment	tiny deposits that settle at the bottom of liquid
sedimentary rock	rock formed from sediment that is compressed over time
seismic wave	force of energy created by an earthquake
tectonic plates	large, slow-moving sections of the Earth's crust
tornado	violent funnel-shaped whirling winds
trench	long, deep ditch in the ocean floor
tributary	river or stream that flows into a larger river
tsunami	long, high sea wave caused by an earthquake

INDEX

Saint Benedict
A Catholic Voluntary Academy
Duffield Road, Darley Abbey
Derby
DE22 1JD